PRINCESS
BERNICE PAUAHI BISHOP

Revised Edition

PRINCESS
BERNICE PAUAHI BISHOP

Revised Edition

Julie Stewart Williams

Illustrated by
Robin Yoko Burningham

Kamehameha Schools Press

Honolulu

KAMEHAMEHA SCHOOLS

First edition copyright © 1992,
Revised edition copyright © 1999
by Kamehameha Schools

Inquiries should be addressed to:

Kamehameha Schools
567 South King Street
Honolulu, Hawai‘i 96813

The paper used in this publication
meets the minimum requirements of
American National Standard for Library Sciences—
Permanence of Paper for Printed Library Materials,
ANSI Z39.48-1992

Printed in the United States of America

ISBN 978-0-87336-057-9

*Cover photo courtesy of Bishop Museum
Ambrotype (electronically retouched) of
Princess Bernice Pauahi Bishop as a young woman*

10 09 08   (rev.) 3 4 5

Dedicated to

Nā Pua a Pauahi

The Children of Pauahi

and to

Gussie Bento

former Coordinator of the

Bernice Pauahi Bishop Heritage Center

on the campus of Kamehameha Schools

Table of Contents

Preface

This book is one of a series originally written by faculty in a Kamehameha reading program. The books were designed to increase students' reading skills and their knowledge of Hawaiian history and culture by focusing on topics such as the Hawaiian monarchy.

Some of these books have been translated from their original English into Hawaiian through the efforts of the staff of the Kamehameha Schools Hawaiian Studies Institute.

We are pleased at the reception both the English and the Hawaiian editions have received from educational and general audiences.

Michael J. Chun, Ph.D.
President
Kamehameha Schools

Acknowledgments

I wish to thank the staff of Kamehameha Schools Intermediate Reading Program for their assistance in the completion of *Princess Bernice Pauahi Bishop*. The first book has been used with students since 1980 when the program's name was "Nā Pua a Pauahi," "The Children of Pauahi." I am grateful to *Naomi Noelani Chun* who helped me all along and also translated an earlier draft into Hawaiian. *Mahalo* to *Kaipo Hale* who reviewed the English-language manuscript for the proper use of Hawaiian. I am also indebted to the graphics unit of Kamehameha Schools Bishop Estate Media and Publications Department for all of their help: to *Robin Yoko Burningham* for her beautiful illustrations, to *Lynn Criss-Fujita* for Pauahi's genealogy, and to *Pat Kaneshiro* for completing the layout. Many thanks to *Lesley Agard* and *Anne Rhea* for editing the English text and seeing it through to the end. *Mahalo a nui loa* to *Hannah Hana Pau* whose expertise in Hawaiian language and diligence resulted in the translation of this book into Hawaiian.

J.S.W.

*Princess Bernice Pauahi Bishop, founder of the
Kamehameha Schools*

Photo courtesy of Bishop Museum

Introduction

"Her love for the young was great, and it was a pretty sight to see her surrounded by a group of children to whose pleasure she was ministering."

Perhaps no other single sentence portrays Pauahi so accurately and so completely as this remembrance of her, published at the time of her death. It captures the essence of the princess and her legacy: love, children, service.

What a beautiful experience to have been in the company of the princess and to have known her in person! May the young readers for whom this book was written be drawn closer to Pauahi. May readers both young and old be inspired to follow her example of service to all.

Pauahi Genealogy

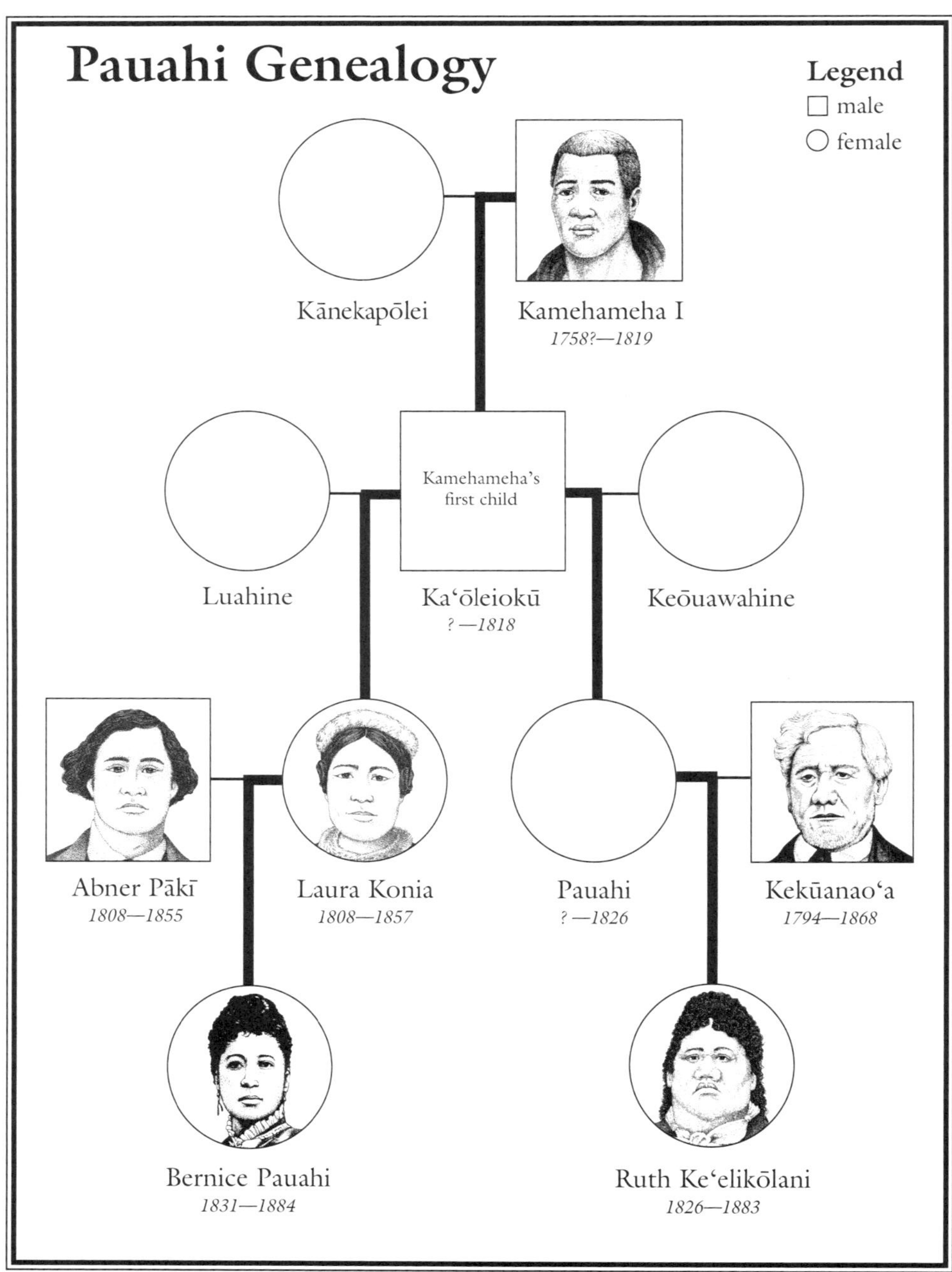

A Princess of Hawai‘i

There once lived in the kingdom of Hawai‘i a beautiful princess who loved her people very much. Her name was Bernice Pauahi Pākī Bishop.

The princess was born in Honolulu on December 19, 1831, at the family's home known as ‘Aikupika, or Egypt. Her parents named her Pauahi after an aunt, her mother's sister.

When Aunt Pauahi was just a baby she was rescued from a fire. Because of that incident she was given the name Pauahi. In Hawaiian, *pau* means "finished" and *ahi* means "fire," Pauahi means "destroyed by fire, burned; to put out a fire."

The father of the princess was High Chief Abner Pākī. He was born on Molokaʻi and was a descendant of the Kamehameha and Kiwalaʻō families of Maui and Hawaiʻi.

Pākī was an advisor and close friend of Kauikeaouli, Kamehameha III. He always accompanied the king on visits to different parts of the kingdom. During his life he held high positions of trust and honor, including being a judge of the supreme court. He was known for his firmness. When he took a stand about something he was immovable, or not able to be moved.

Pākī was six feet four inches tall and weighed about three hundred pounds. He was a man of great strength. One day the horses pulling his carriage became frightened and tried to run away. Instead of using the reins to slow them down he threw himself across the horses and held them with his bare hands until they quieted down.

Pauahi's father, High Chief Abner Pākī (1808–1855)
Photo courtesy of Bishop Museum

The mother of the princess was High Chiefess Laura Konia. Her parents were Luahine and Ka'ōleiokū, the first son of Kamehameha I. Konia was Kamehameha's granddaughter. Pauahi was his great-granddaughter.

Konia was known for her kindness and hospitality, or generous treatment of guests or strangers. Pauahi inherited her gracious manner.

When Kamehameha III formed his first council of high chiefs he selected Konia as one of his advisors. She served as a member of the legislature from 1840 to 1847.

Pauahi's mother, High Chiefess Laura Konia (1808–1857)
Photo courtesy of Bishop Museum

Pākī and Konia loved their baby daughter. She was their first child. Yet she would live with them for just a few days. It was the custom to let a relative *hānai,* or adopt, your child. Konia had promised Pauahi to her Aunt Kīna'u.

Kīna'u was the eldest daughter of Kamehameha. She was one of the highest ranking chiefesses of that time. When Ka'ahumanu died in 1832 Kīna'u succeeded her as the *kuhina nui,* or co-ruler, with Kamehameha III. Her husband was Kekūanao'a, the governor of O'ahu and a judge.

Kīna‘u (1805?–1839), hānai *mother of Pauahi*

Photo courtesy of Bishop Museum

At the time of Pauahi's birth Kīna'u had three sons,
all of whom were *hānai* by other relatives. Now,
most of all, Kīna'u wanted a girl. She asked Pākī
and Konia for their baby daughter. And, as was the
custom, they consented.

The little princess was less than a week old when
she was given to her great-aunt Kīna'u. Kīna'u and
Kekūanao'a became the foster parents of Pauahi. For
the next seven and a half years they would love the
little princess and care for her as their very own.

Kekūanao‘a (1794–1868), hānai *father of Pauahi, with
daughter Victoria Kamāmalu (1838–1866)*

Photo courtesy of Bishop Museum

Altogether Kīna‘u and Kekūanao‘a had five children. They were David Kamehameha, Moses Kekūaiwa, Lot Kapuāiwa, Alexander Liholiho and Victoria Kamāmalu. Kamehameha III took Alexander as his *hānai* son.

Pauahi was two years old when Alexander was born. She was seven when Kīna‘u gave birth to Victoria on November 1, 1838. But a sad thing happened a few months later. On April 4, 1839, Kīna‘u died of mumps. She was only about thirty-four years old.

First row: Queen Kalama, Kamehameha III, Victoria Kamāmalu;
second row: Alexander Liholiho and Lot Kapuāiwa

Photo courtesy of Bishop Museum

Meanwhile Pākī and Konia had taken as their *hānai*
child a baby girl who was born on September 2,
1838. The child's mother was Keohokālole. Her father
was Kapaʻakea. Kīnaʻu named the little girl Liliʻu,
"smarting or painful," Kamakaʻeha, "the sore eye,"
after a time when Kīnaʻu herself was ill with a
headache and sore eyes.

Lili'u Kamaka'eha (1838–1917), hānai *sister of Pauahi*

Photo courtesy of Bishop Museum

Now with Kīnaʻu gone Pākī and Konia wanted to get their own daughter back. At first Kekūanaoʻa would not let Pauahi go. Finally he gave in and Pauahi returned to live with her parents and her foster sister Liliʻu Kamakaʻeha. Years later Liliʻu became Queen Liliʻuokalani, the last monarch of the Hawaiian kingdom.

Hānai *sisters, Pauahi and Liliʻu*
Photo courtesy of Bishop Museum

A School
for Royal Children

While Pauahi was growing up the king of Hawai'i was Kauikeaouli, Kamehameha III. He was a son of Kamehameha and Keōpuōlani and the younger brother of Liholiho, Kamehameha II.

Kamehameha III wanted his people to be educated. He said, "My kingdom shall be a kingdom of learning." He established schools throughout the islands so that his people could learn to read and write. He believed firmly that knowledge and skills were required for the survival of the kingdom.

Kauikeaouli, Kamehameha III (1814–1854)
Photo courtesy of Bishop Museum

Kamehameha III had a special concern for the future rulers of Hawai'i. Foreigners, or people from other countries, were coming to the islands. Their ways were different and they spoke different languages. Kauikeaouli realized that if a king or queen was to rule wisely he or she needed to be educated about many things.

Kīna'u, the king and the chiefs wanted a school just for the young *ali'i,* or chiefs and chiefesses. At this school the future rulers would learn the English language. They would also get to know and understand the ways of the foreigners.

The king and chiefs hired Amos Starr Cooke and his wife, Juliette Montague Cooke, to set up a school and teach their royal children. The Cookes were Christian missionaries who had sailed to Hawai'i from Boston, Massachusetts, in 1837.

While the new school was being built the children went to a day school in a temporary classroom. There were six students: Pauahi, Moses, Lot, Alexander, Lunalilo and Kaliokalani, an older brother of Lili'u. Their first day was June 13, 1839. Over the next ten years ten more children would enter the school.

Amos Starr Cooke (1810–1871)
with daughter Mary Annis
Photo courtesy of Mission Houses Museum

Juliette Montague Cooke (1812–1896)
with son Amos Francis
Photo courtesy of Mission Houses Museum

A year later, in May 1840, the new school was ready. It was built near the site of the present state capitol. The building was square shaped with a courtyard in the center. It had a large classroom, kitchen, dining room, sitting room, parlor and several bedrooms. Next to the building was a large garden with walkways neatly arranged and lined with flowers.

The new school was a boarding school. Here the students would live and learn all year round.

The Royal School
Photo courtesy of Bishop Museum

The school was first called the "Chiefs' Children's School." In 1846 its name was changed to the "Royal School."

Pauahi was now eight and a half years old. The Chiefs' Children's School became her new home. There she would receive what was described as "training of the head, the hand, the heart and the home." There she would live until the age of eighteen.

Sixteen young *ali'i* were taught at the Royal
School. Eight were chiefs and eight were chiefesses.
Four of the boys grew up to become kings. They
were Alexander Liholiho (Kamehameha IV), Lot
Kapuāiwa (Kamehameha V), William Lunalilo and
David Kalākaua. Two of the girls became queens:
Emma, as the wife of Kamehameha IV, and Lili'u,
who reigned as Lili'uokalani.

Alexander Liholiho
Kamehameha IV
Emma
Lot Kapuāiwa
Kamehameha V

William Lunalilo
David Kalākaua
Liliʻuokalani

A Gifted Pupil

When Pauahi and the other young *ali'i* entered the Chiefs' Children's School the only language they knew was their native language, Hawaiian. Now they had to learn to speak, read and write in a second language, English.

All of the children's instruction was in English. Their classes included algebra, arithmetic, astronomy, chemistry, geography, geometry, history, literature and spelling. They also had lessons in music and painting.

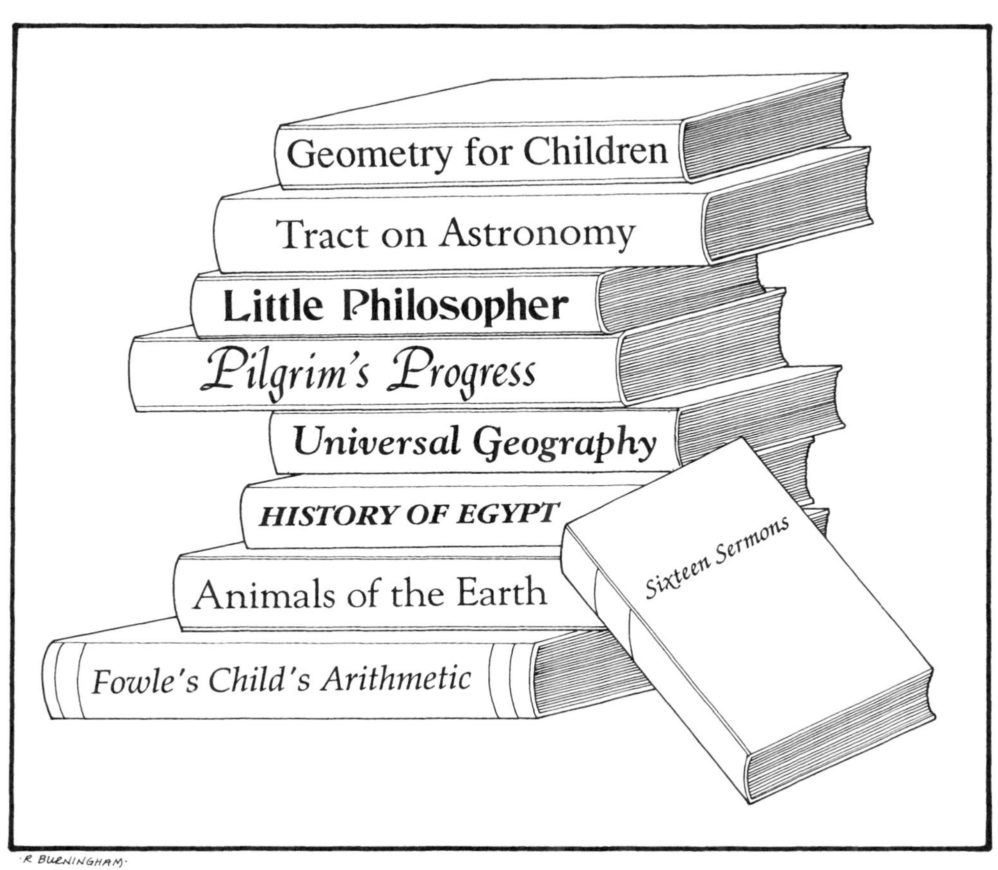

Some of the textbooks used by the royal children

Another change for the children was that their many *kahu,* or attendants, could not stay with them at the school. Pauahi had several *kahu.* Alexander had at least thirty. The *kahu* did everything for their young *aliʻi.* Now the children would learn to do things for themselves. John Papa ʻĪʻī and his wife, Sarah, were assistant teachers. Mr. ʻĪʻī also served as the official *kahu* for the school.

The students had to get used to a daily routine plus the many rules of behavior made by the Cookes. The boys had the most problems adjusting to life in a boarding school.

But even Pauahi broke some rules. Once she was caught laughing in church. She also threw dirt into a neighbor's yard. Another time Moses, Lot and Alexander were caught eating fish and *poi* in her room.

John 'I'i, kahu at the Chiefs' Children's School
Photo courtesy of Bishop Museum

The children spent much of their evenings reading aloud to one another and writing in the journals they were required to keep. The earliest example of Pauahi's writing in English was her journal entry for January 11, 1843. She was eleven years old.

> "We had a school as usal we did not got our lesson in arithmetic and this afternoon in geography we have not recied grammar. After prayer we went out to esercis on the when we were playing very happy then Moses Lot & Alexander came with us to play the Emma felt down and heart her limp."

Jan 11
1843—

This morning I did not write my journal ... because it is to late to write and so we had a writing school. We had a school as usal we did not get our lesson in arithmetic and this afternoon in geography we have not recad grammar After prayer we went to out to exercis on the when we were playing very happy then Moses Lot &, Alexander came with us to play the Emma fell down and heart her limp.

Jan, 12
1843—

After dinner Abigail William & I went to play in the carpenter hous we told William I to go and get all his handerchef and the bell rung for school This noon we ... about Greece and is was very ... indeed

Pauahi's handwritten journal entries for
January 11 and 12, 1843

Photo courtesy of Bishop Museum

Swimming and horseback riding were everyone's favorite sports. But, judging from her journal entries, Pauahi seems to have enjoyed horseback riding the most. Sometimes everyone sailed to another island for a short visit or traveled to other places on O'ahu. They also took part in community activities. They attended important ceremonies such as the restoration of the Hawaiian flag by Admiral Richard Thomas on July 13, 1843.

Pauahi enjoyed horseback riding

Prayers and devotions were held every morning
and evening. On Sundays the children marched in a
procession to Kawaiaha‘o Church. They marched by
twos, a boy and girl side by side with the eldest
taking the lead. They attended services—sitting near
the king's pew. They also sang in a choir with
Pauahi leading the singing.

Kawaiaha'o Church
Photo courtesy of Bishop Museum

Pauahi had a wide variety of interests and was very eager to learn. She was an excellent writer. She enjoyed painting. She loved music and played the piano and melodeon. It was she who taught the younger girls to play the piano and to sing.

In addition Pauahi learned to cook, clean house, wash and sew her own clothes. She was very fond of children and often looked after the younger ones.

Pauahi loved flowers and the outdoors. Her journal entry on January 31, 1843, shows how observant she was of nature, even at the young age of eleven.

> "This morning when we arose the skies was black cloud and the wink was blowing hard. After breakfast it commenced raining and it had been raining all day. Of course it has not been pleasant to there abrod but vegetation is greatly refreshed and we rejoice with the tree and the grass."

On December 19, 1843, Pauahi celebrated her twelfth birthday with friends who had come to see her. Mr. Southy of the English ship *Champion* brought her a beautiful music box. The guests played games with the children. Mrs. Cooke served cakes, raisins, nuts and lemonade.

Soon there were more surprises. Someone knocked loudly on the front door and then the serenading began. A group of German sailors sang several songs, all in the German language. After the singing the door was opened. The sailors entered with an elegant fruit cake beautifully decorated with colored frosting. In the center of the cake was the name "PAUAHI."

Many people made it a point to visit the Royal School. Mrs. Cooke was known as a very gracious hostess. Besides the parents, visitors included the king, other *ali'i,* foreign officials, businessmen and ships' officers. They found the children to be very friendly and interesting. The children, in turn, enjoyed the visitors, who often brought them gifts.

Pauahi was very much at ease in the presence of guests. She was said to have been "an interesting and brilliant conversationalist, ready to talk upon almost any topic."

Pauahi's journal entry on October 2, 1844, tells about her day and three rules for good manners. It also shows the improvement in her writing.

"This has been a pleasant day. We had a good school this afternoon. I did few sums in my slate of Written Arithmetic. After dinner we went out in the woods to make a bon–fire. At four o'clock Mrs. Cooke rung the bell for us to come in and wright our journals. Nobody called on us today.

(1) Speak not too loud not to low.

(2) Answer not one that speaks to you till he has done.

(3) Speak not without Sir or some title of respect which is due to him to whom you speak."

Mr. Gorham O. Gilman, a friend and businessman, described Pauahi when she was about fourteen years old.

> "She is now a young lady and combines a well
> cultivated mind with much grace of person…
> she would win golden opinions in any circle.
> She is of middle statue, of light complexion, and
> of much ease of manners, plays and sings prettily,
> and will adorn any station she may fill in her
> native islands, being probably the best educated
> of all the Hawaiian girls."

Princess Pauahi, age fifteen
Photo courtesy of Bishop Museum

That Pauahi was indeed a gifted and well-rounded pupil is very clear in a letter written by her teacher. Mrs. Cooke wrote to her sister about her favorite pupil, "Miss Bernice."

> "She is a most lovely girl—lovely in feature, form, and disposition. Extremely prudent, seldom giving cause for any reproof. She reads to me every day an hour. She is now reading *Coelebs in Search of a Wife*. She has just finished the *History of Egypt*—is very fond of reading, likes history and is very well versed in it for a girl of her age—she is fifteen—plays and sings well, paints prettily, works worsted, makes her own dresses, is now studying chemistry and Euclid…. I wish you could know her, you would love her…"

Deeply in Love

One day early in the year 1847 a young man visited the Royal School. He was an American businessman from Glens Falls, New York, who arrived in Hawai'i in 1846. He met the young princess. She was about 16 years old and very pretty. Her foster sister Lili'u described her as "…one of the most beautiful girls I ever saw; the vision of her loveliness can never be effaced from remembrance; like a striking picture once seen, it is stamped upon memory's page forever."

It wasn't long before the young man was calling upon the princess every evening. The two fell deeply in love. The American was Charles Reed Bishop.

The princess and Mr. Bishop were married the evening of June 4, 1850, in the parlor of the Royal School. Pauahi was eighteen years old and Charles was twenty-eight. The bride wore a gown of white muslin and a *lei* of *pīkake,* or jasmine. Only a few people were present. After the ceremony Mrs. Cooke served tea. Everything was over in an hour. The wedding was quick and simple.

Pauahi's parents opposed the marriage and did not attend the wedding. They had hoped their daughter would marry Lot Kapuāiwa, who later became Kamehameha V.

Wedding picture of Mr. and Mrs. Charles Reed Bishop, 1850
Photo courtesy of Bishop Museum

The Bishops spent their honeymoon in Kōloa on the island of Kaua‘i. After three weeks they returned to O‘ahu and lived in a small house in downtown Honolulu. Their marriage was a happy marriage.

A year passed, and Pākī and Konia began to change their mind about Charles. They got to know him and found him to be wise, honest and a devoted husband. In time they accepted Pauahi's marriage to Charles. This made the princess very happy.

Princess Bernice Pauahi Bishop, age nineteen
Photo courtesy of Bishop Museum

On June 13, 1855, Pākī died. He left everything he owned to Pauahi. This included nearly 6,000 acres of land on Oʻahu and his beautiful home, Haleakalā. Haleakalā was located on two acres of land, where ʻAikupika once stood, *ma uka* of the present intersection of King and Bishop Streets.

The Bishops then moved into Haleakalā and lived with Konia and Liliʻu. Just two years later Konia died. Like Pākī, she left Pauahi all of her lands—which amounted to over 10,000 acres. These lands were in Kona on the island of Hawaiʻi, on Oʻahu and Kauaʻi.

Haleakalā, built by Pākī and left to Pauahi in 1855
Photo courtesy of Hawai'i State Archives

Princess Bernice Pauahi Bishop, age twenty-three
Photo courtesy of Bishop Museum

Of Service to All

Mr. and Mrs. Bishop became the social and cultural leaders of Honolulu. People gathered in their home, Haleakalā, for conversation, meetings, music recitals, reading and receptions. Children came for piano lessons with Pauahi. Both Pauahi and Charles enjoyed reading and their home was filled with books.

The Bishops entertained visitors from Japan and England and other foreign countries. They welcomed high officials as well as little children. There were tea parties, dances and croquet games. Pauahi was known as a very gracious hostess and no guest was turned away.

Princess Bernice Pauahi Bishop, age thirty-five
Photo courtesy of Bishop Museum

Charles Reed Bishop, age forty-five
Photo courtesy of Bishop Museum

While Charles was busy with his government responsibilities and business career Pauahi managed Haleakalā. She was an excellent manager. Everything she did seemed to be marked by prudence, or wisdom, and good judgement.

The Bishops had at least thirty *kahu,* or attendants. These *kahu* and their families lived in two low buildings on the grounds. Even though Pauahi had many attendants she still helped with the housework. She was strict about work which was sloppy or carelessly done. She was also strict about being prompt and finishing work on time.

Pauahi was frugal, or not wasteful. For example
she gave sewing lessons to the women and she
taught them to save every bit of basting thread
so it could be used over and over again. She still
continued to sew some of her own clothes.

The grounds of Haleakalā were full of beautiful
flowers, shrubs, and trees. Pauahi loved flowers.
Although she had well-trained gardeners she was
often found working herself among the plants. She
enjoyed sending gifts of plants and flowers which she
had raised to her friends and neighbors. Very often
she would gather flowers to take to people who
were sick.

On the day of Pauahi's birth her *ʻiewe,* or afterbirth, was buried in the front yard of ʻAikupika. It was the custom to bury the *ʻiewe* under a tree but there was no suitable tree growing in the yard. So a young tamarind tree was planted over the afterbirth to protect it. Because the tree was planted in honor of Pauahi, it was *kapu,* or sacred.

The tamarind tree now was quite big. Under this tree Pauahi frequently met and counseled her people. Sometimes she would sit for hours listening to them. They would tell her their problems or feelings. She would give them advice or try to comfort them. She would think of ways to help them solve their problems.

Pauahi with her people under the tamarind tree
planted on the day she was born

The princess was able to bring together the two cultures in which she was raised: the western Christian way and that of a Hawaiian *ali'i*. She was a devout, or deeply religious, Christian. She taught a Sunday School class at Kawaiaha'o Church and was a faithful teacher of children for many years. A memorial tablet has been placed on the wall above the pew where Pauahi and her parents once sat.

As would any true Hawaiian *ali'i,* Pauahi served her people well. She counseled them and helped them in many ways. Very often she sent gifts or went to the homes of people in need. She would visit a person who was ill and prepare a meal for that person.

Princess Bernice Pauahi Bishop, age forty
Photo courtesy of Bishop Museum

"No, no! Not me!"

Kamehameha V, Lot Kapuāiwa, ruled from 1863 to 1872. Just before he died he sent for Pauahi. He had something very important to tell her.

With Pauahi at his bedside, the king said, "I wish you to take my place, to be my successor..."

Pauahi was startled and replied, "No, no! Not me! Don't think of me!"

Lot insisted, saying, "...I think it best for my people and my nation."

But Pauahi said, "Oh, no! Do not think of me. There are others; there is your sister [Ruth], it is hers by right.... There is the Queen, Emma; she has been a Queen once."

The princess could have become queen of Hawai'i but she refused. And Lot died without naming a successor.

Lot Kapuāiwa, Kamehameha V (1830–1872)
Photo courtesy of Bishop Museum

To Faraway Places

During the years 1875 and 1876 the Bishops traveled. They toured the United States and Canada. They traveled to England, Ireland and Scotland. They visited many places all over Europe.

Pauahi wrote letters to her cousin Cordie who was housesitting at Haleakalā. Cousin Cordie, Mrs. William Allen of California, was Mr. Bishop's niece. In her letters Pauahi described the places she visited, the people she met and the things she did. There was so much to see and do.

Mr. and Mrs. Charles Reed Bishop in San Francisco, 1876
Photo courtesy of Bishop Museum

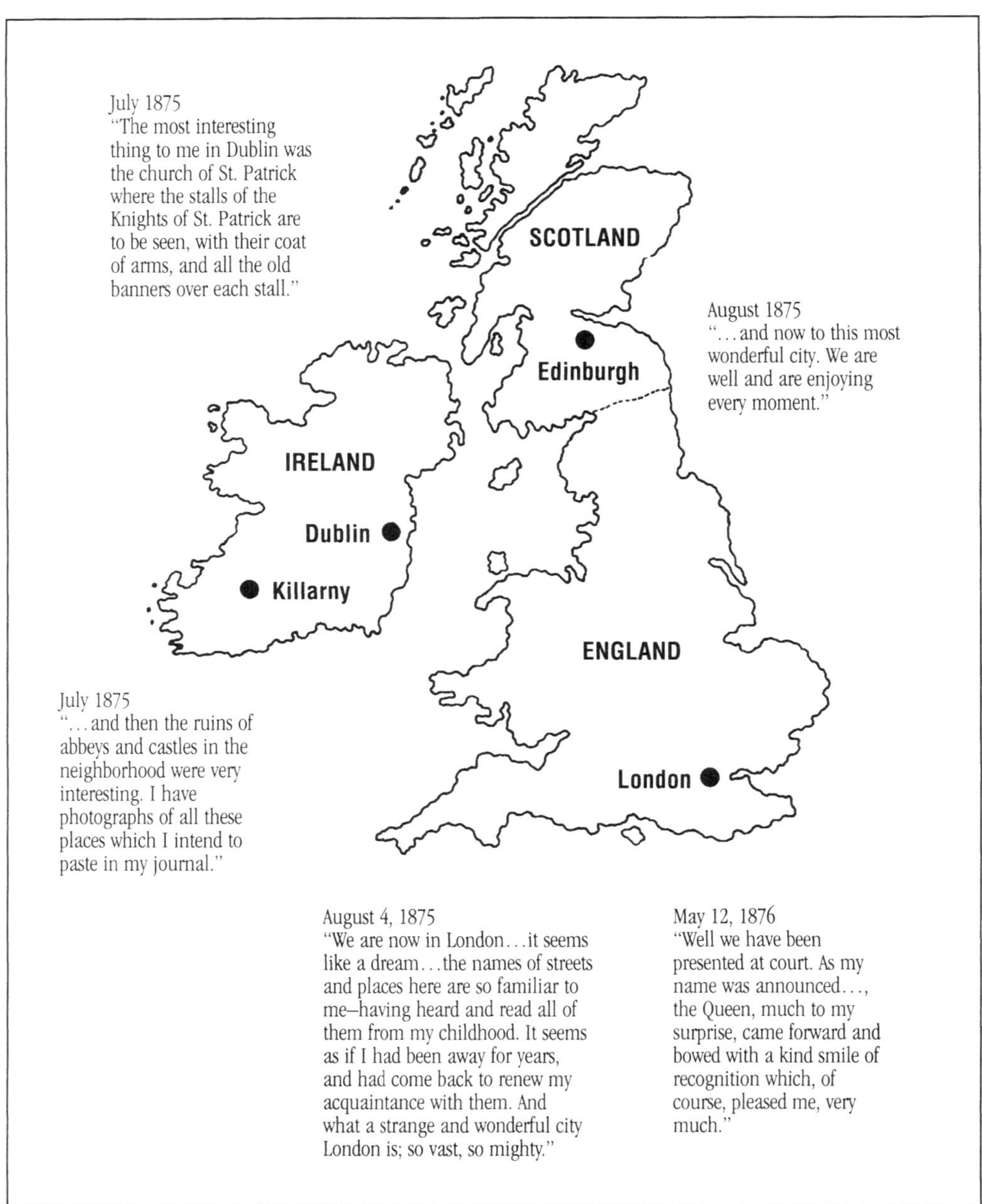

Excerpts from letters written by Pauahi to her cousin Cordie

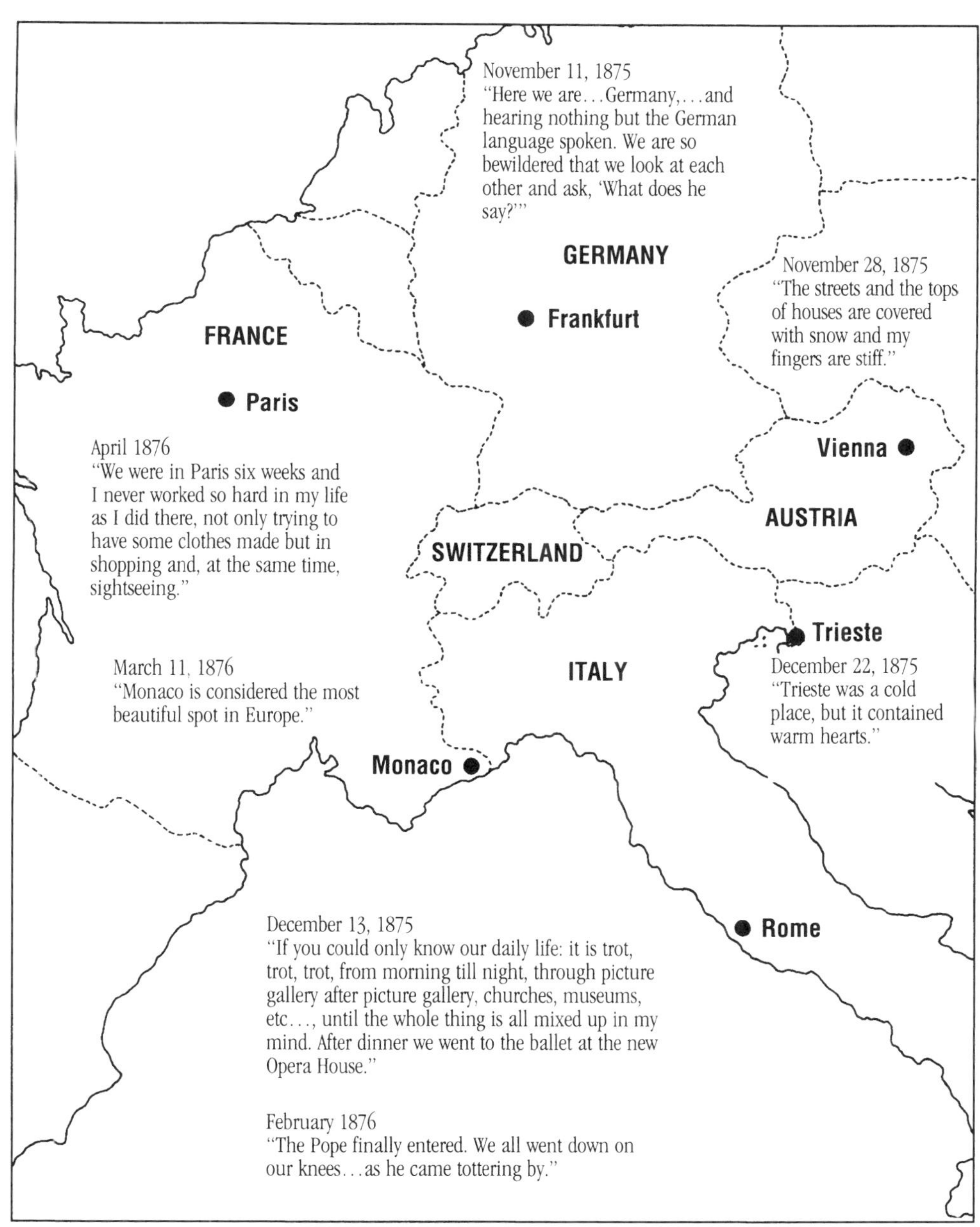

November 11, 1875
"Here we are…Germany,…and hearing nothing but the German language spoken. We are so bewildered that we look at each other and ask, 'What does he say?'"

GERMANY

Frankfurt

November 28, 1875
"The streets and the tops of houses are covered with snow and my fingers are stiff."

FRANCE

Paris

April 1876
"We were in Paris six weeks and I never worked so hard in my life as I did there, not only trying to have some clothes made but in shopping and, at the same time, sightseeing."

Vienna

AUSTRIA

SWITZERLAND

March 11, 1876
"Monaco is considered the most beautiful spot in Europe."

Trieste

ITALY

December 22, 1875
"Trieste was a cold place, but it contained warm hearts."

Monaco

December 13, 1875
"If you could only know our daily life: it is trot, trot, trot, from morning till night, through picture gallery after picture gallery, churches, museums, etc…, until the whole thing is all mixed up in my mind. After dinner we went to the ballet at the new Opera House."

Rome

February 1876
"The Pope finally entered. We all went down on our knees…as he came tottering by."

Cousin Ruth Keʻelikōlani

Pauahi and her cousin Ruth Keʻelikōlani were very close. They were like sisters. Pauahi was named after Ruth's mother.

Years earlier, in 1862, a boy was born to Ruth and her husband Isaac Young Davis. Ruth gave her baby to Pauahi and Charles, who had no children of their own. They loved their *hānai* son very much. His name was Keolaokalani. Happiness turned to sadness when the little boy became ill and died before he was even one year old.

Ruth built an elaborate mansion on Emma Street which she named Keōua Hale. After its completion in early 1883 a housewarming *lūʻau* was held on her birthday, February 9. However Ruth never stayed in her new house. She preferred the *lānai* of her old place nearby.

Princess Ruth Keʻelikolani (1826–1883)
Photo courtesy of Bishop Museum

The day after the *lū'au,* Ruth became ill. She was taken to Kailua, Kona, where her doctor thought her health might improve. She stayed in her grass house on the grounds of Hulihe'e Palace. But on May 24, 1883, at the age of fifty-seven, she died of heart disease. Pauahi was at her bedside.

Ruth's body was brought back to Keōua Hale for the period of mourning, which lasted three weeks. Pauahi was very sad and very tired. Soon her health began to weaken. Before long she became seriously ill.

Princess Ruth Ke'elikōlani left the bulk of her estate to Pauahi. This included Keōua Hale and about 350,000 acres of Kamehameha lands.

Keōua Hale, Princess Ruth Keʻelikōlani's mansion
Photo courtesy of Bishop Museum

"*Aloha*, Pauahi!"

The princess was ill with cancer for several months. In April 1884, heeding her doctor's advice, she sailed to San Francisco where she underwent an operation. She returned to Honolulu in June. She spent some time at her summer home in Waikīkī near the present site of the Royal Hawaiian Hotel.

But Pauahi's condition did not improve. Instead it got worse and, on October 9, she was taken to Keōua Hale. On October 16, 1884, she lay unconscious with Charles, her husband of over thirty-four years, at her bedside. The rains fell steadily. Then, at twelve minutes past noon, Princess Pauahi died. She was fifty-two years of age.

Princess Bernice Pauahi Bishop (1831–1884)
Photo courtesy of Bishop Museum

During the period of mourning it rained almost continuously. But at the final service on October 30 "the clouds lifted, the sky became clear and the sun shone brightly."

Pauahi's body was placed in a casket made of *koa* and *kou,* two beautiful Hawaiian woods. On the lid was a silver shield with the following inscription:

THE HONORABLE
BERNICE PAUAHI BISHOP
DAUGHTER OF THE
CHIEFS A. PAKI AND L. KONIA
AND WIFE OF THE HONORABLE
CHARLES R. BISHOP
BORN DECEMBER 19, 1831
DIED OCTOBER 16TH, 1884

In a long procession of over nine hundred people and seventy-five carriages, the cortege proceeded from Keōua Hale on Emma Street to Beretania Street and up Nuʻuanu Street to Mauna ʻAla, the site of the Royal Mausoleum. There Pauahi was laid to rest in the Kamehameha crypt, or underground burial vault.

Tombstone for the Kamehameha crypt at Mauna'ala

Kamehameha V had offered the throne to Pauahi. But she turned it down. Perhaps it was just as well. The words of the Reverend J.A. Cruzan tell us why:

"The last and the best of the Kamehamehas lies in her last long sleep. Refusing a crown, she lived that which she was—crowned. Refusing to rule her people, she did what was better, she served them, and in no way so grandly as by her example…"

Pauahi lived longer than the other direct descendants of Kamehameha I, her great-grandfather. Her death ended an important chapter in the history of the Hawaiian kingdom.

"Kamehameha, King of the Sandwich Isles"
by Louis Choris

Portrait courtesy of Honolulu Academy of Arts

Legacy of a Princess

As the last direct royal descendant of Kamehameha I, Pauahi inherited many acres of land from her cousin Ruth. Her parents and her aunt ʻAkahi, who died in 1877, also left her their lands. Altogether, she had about 375,500 acres.

What was to become of Pauahi's large estate? The Bishops loved children, yet they had none of their own. Pauahi had no children to inherit her lands.

A year before she died Pauahi wrote Article
Thirteen of her will. She directed the trustees of
her estate

> "...to erect and maintain in the Hawaiian Islands
> two schools, each for boarding and day scholars,
> one for boys and one for girls, to be known as,
> and called the Kamehameha Schools."

Pauahi also stated,

> "I desire my Trustees to provide first and chiefly
> a good education in the common English
> branches, and also instruction in morals and in
> such knowledge as may tend to make good and
> industrious men and women."

And that is how Kamehameha Schools came to
be! Pauahi's concern for her people culminated, or
reached its peak, in the founding of the schools
which she named after her great-grandfather
Kamehameha I.

The Kamehameha Schools' campus
Photo by Bruce Lum, KSBE

Pauahi inherited about 375,500 acres of land. Later some land was given away, condemned or sold. About 366,000 acres remain. These form the corpus, or core asset, of the Bernice Pauahi Bishop Estate. Income, or money earned, comes from charging rent to those who use the land. Income has also come from selling land and investing some of the money.

Bishop Estate pays for most of the costs of educating Hawaiian boys and girls enrolled in Kamehameha Schools Bernice Pauahi Bishop Estate's educational programs. These students enjoy the advantages provided by Pauahi's estate.

Kamehameha Schools began its education of Hawaiian boys and girls in 1887 and is intended to continue "in perpetuity," or forever. Thus there will be no end to the number of children who can be called "the *hānai* sons and daughters" of Bernice Pauahi and Charles Reed Bishop.

He Inoa No Pauahi

(Pauahi's favorite *mele inoa,* or name song)

1.

Honi ana i ke anu, i ka mea huʻihuʻi,

Huʻi hewa i ka ʻili, i ka ua Pōʻaihala,

Lei ana i ka mokihana, i ka wewehi o Kaiona,

Līhau pue i ke anu, hauʻoki o Kaleponi.

2.

Hiaʻai ka welina, ka neneʻe a ka ʻōhelopapa,

Pupua i ka noe, mōhāhā i ke anu,

Noho nō me ka ʻanoʻi, ka manaʻo iā loko,

ʻO loko hana nui, pau ʻole i ke ana ʻia.

3.

A ka wailele o Niakala, ʻike i ka wai anuenue,

I ka pōʻaiʻai a ka ʻohu, hāliʻi paʻa i laila,

Pue ana i ka ʻehu wai, pupuʻu i ke koʻekoʻe,

Eia iho ka mehana o ka poli o Hiʻilei.

4.

E ō e ka wahine hele lā o Kaiona,

Alualu wailiʻulā o ke kaha pua ʻōhai,

ʻO ka ua lani pōlua, pō anu o ke Koʻolau,

Kuʻu hoa o ka malu kī, malu kukui o Kahoʻiwai.

(Kaiona—a goddess of Mt. Kaʻala)

(Kahoʻiwai—a place in Mānoa Valley)

A Name Chant
In Honor Of Pauahi

English translation

1.

Braving the cold and all things with chill,
Biting as they strive, braving also the rain,
The glory of our land, adorned with *mokihana,*
Is radiant in the snow of icy California.

2.

Yearning for her, clinging closely as the mountain vine
Spreads and unfolds despite the mist and cold,
There she stayed in greatest love, possessed of hidden
    thoughts,
Exalted, high, never to be measured.

3.

At the falls of Niagara where she saw the rainbow's arch,
In the all-surrounding mist, shrouded tight about it,
Chilled she was by the water vapor, and shriveled up
    with dampness.
There she found the warmth aglowing in the bosom
    of Hiʻilei.

4.

Respond, O lady in the sunshine of Kaiona,
Who seeks the mirages amid the *ʻōhai* of the plain,
In the pouring, the cold rain of Koʻolau,
My companion in the sheltering *kī* and *kukui* of Kahoʻiwai.

Pauahi ʻo Kalani

Composed by Queen Liliʻuokalani in honor of her foster sister, Pauahi (A *mele* that tells about Pauahi's enjoyment of nature and her concern for her people.)

1.
Noho ana ka wahine i ke anu o Mānā,
Mahalo i ka nani nohea o ka nahele.

2.
Ua ʻike i nā paia ʻaʻala hoʻi o Puna,
Ua lei nā maile o Panaʻewa hoʻi.

3.
Hoʻi ana nō naʻe ke aloha i nā kini.
I ke one hānau i ka home i ke kaona.

(Chorus)
E ola ʻo Kalani e Pauahi lani nui,
A kau i ka pua ʻaneʻane,
E ola ʻo Kalani e Pauahi lani nui,
E ola loa no a kau i ka wēkiu.

Pauahi, the Royal One

English translation

1.

There she stays, our lady, in the cool clime of Mānā,
Admiring all its beauties, the glories of the forest.

2.

She has sensed the fragrant spices of Puna's bowers;
She has worn the many *maile* from Pana'ewa's forests.

3.

But her thoughts turn ever to love her kin;
To her home, her birthplace, she now is returning.

(Chorus)
Live, Oh Highness, Pauahi, royal great!
'Til time shall no more
Live, Oh Highness, Pauahi, royal great!
Live long, in truth, supreme in excellence!

Princess Bernice Pauahi Bishop, age thirty-three
Photo courtesy of Bishop Museum

Bibliography

Bailey, Paul. *Those Kings and Queens of Old Hawai‘i.*
Los Angeles: Westernlore Books, 1975.

Bishop, Bernice Pauahi. Journal, January 1843–May
1844. Bernice Pauahi Bishop Museum Archives.
Honolulu.

Bishop, Bernice Pauahi. Journal, June 1844–October
1846. Bernice Pauahi Bishop Museum Archives.
Honolulu.

Black, Cobey, and Kathleen D. Mellen. *Princess
Pauahi Bishop and Her Legacy.* Honolulu:
Kamehameha Schools Press, 1965.

Curtis, Caroline. *Builders of Hawaii.* Honolulu:
Kamehameha Schools Press, 1966.

Founder's Day Book. Honolulu: Kamehameha Schools
Press, 1962.

Holt, John Dominis. *The Art of Featherwork in Old Hawai'i.* Honolulu: Topgallant Publishing Co., Ltd., 1985.

Kanahele, George Hu'eu Sanford. *Pauahi: The Kamehameha Legacy.* Honolulu: Kamehameha Schools Press, 1986.

Kent, Harold Winfield. *An Album of Likenesses.* Honolulu: Bernice Pauahi Bishop Museum, 1972.

Krout, Mary H. *The Memoirs of Hon. Bernice Pauahi Bishop.* New York: The Knickerbocker Press, 1908. Reprint, Honolulu: Kamehameha Schools Press, 1958.

Liliuokalani. *Hawaii's Story by Hawaii's Queen.* Boston: Lothrop Lee & Shepard Company, 1898. Reprint, Rutland, Vt., and Tokyo: Charles E. Tuttle Company, Inc., 1964.

Richards, Mary H. *The Hawaiian Chiefs' Children's School, 1839–1850.* Honolulu: 1937. Reprint, Rutland, Vt., and Tokyo: Charles E. Tuttle Company, 1970.

Zambucka, Kristin. *The High Chiefess Ruth Keelikolani.* Honolulu: Mana Publishing Co., 1977.

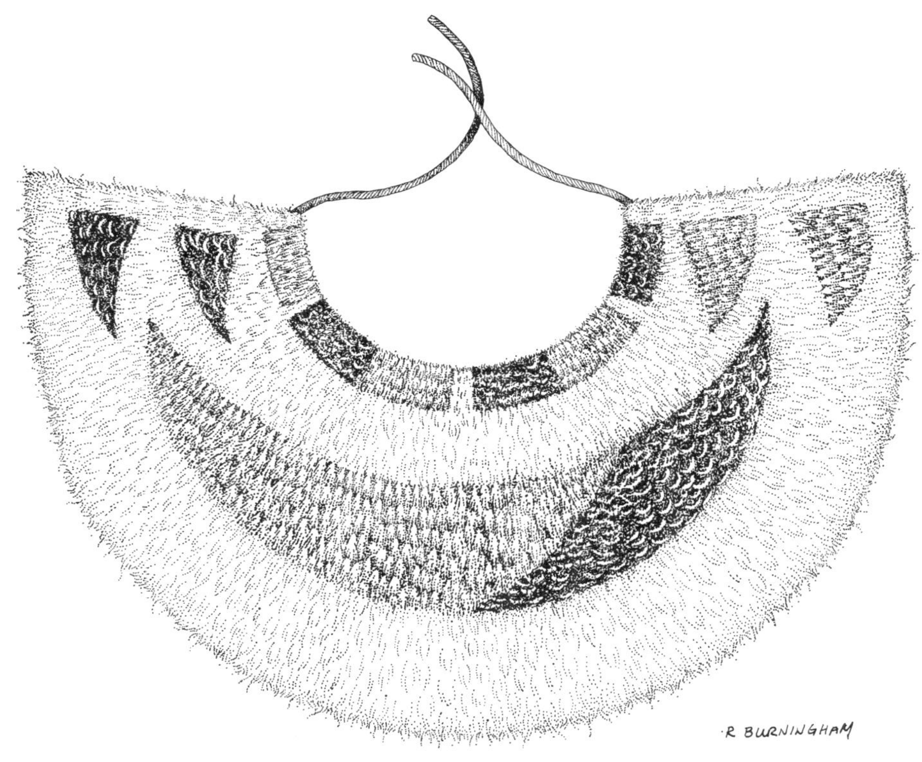

Pauahi's yellow, red and black feather cape—worn on special occasions